Also the Gentle World

poems by

Robert Morrison Randolph

Finishing Line Press
Georgetown, Kentucky

Also the Gentle World

ACKNOWLEDGMENTS

No poem in this book has been published previously, but this is a personal
acknowledgment. The girl on the cover is my daughter Brittany, one of my
four children to whom these poems are dedicated. Brittany passed away in
her early thirties but in her life understood the gentle world. I acknowledge
her ongoing profound influence on all of us who knew her and loved her.

Publisher: Leah Huete de Maines
Editor: Christen Kincaid
Cover Art: Robert Morrison Randolph
Author Photo: Robert Morrison Randolph
Cover Design: Elizabeth Maines McCleavy

Order online: www.finishinglinepress.com
        also available on amazon.com

Author inquiries and mail orders:
Finishing Line Press
PO Box 1626
Georgetown, Kentucky 40324
USA

for
Anna, Britt, Eli, and Pilar

1

     Swallows must have
haiku in their bones
              to turn in flight so deeply
       and simply.

2

We talked by the river;
no word was easy.
             We stared at the water
    as if we had anchors

3

       The old man plays
violin outside at night
           and the stars open
     their glass doors.

4

        I walk in fresh snow
out into the pasture
              to look at the moon
       in its jar of light.

5

      She saw an osprey
fly low in the rain,
           and she played dulcimer
      with her eyes closed.

6

     In this light,
things listen;
          my lace curtains
    call to the moon.

7

Within
the moth's wing
         a distant sea
    breaks on stone.

8

It is not the old
wooden wharf itself,
                but its *silence*
        in today's rain.

9

        The teacup my mother left
lifts me by my thumb and first finger
              to our happy talks at the table
      when she was here.

10

        The empty flag pole
    against winter sky,
                one brush stroke
        on rice paper

11

    He walks
with such selfhood, as if
        having walked through
    a thousand mirrors.

12

        That wagon wheel
leaning against the barn
                years ago rolled
      out of its heart's dream.

13

       Those barn door
hinges are so old;
             they have forgotten
     the moon.

14

        I drift out
   through the window
             and the snow
      falls through me.

15

       The pianist lifts her hands
after the last note,
              and in my bones the moon
      shines on the sea.

16-About Love

Every feather of every bird
is one more word in the language of life.
It all speaks into the center--which is
this moment--and here we are alive in it.
Let's listen, give thanks, create beauty,
and learn how to love for real.

Robert Morrison Randolph's roots go back to a childhood in which the family drew water from a well and heated three rooms with a kerosene stove. From his parents he learned about resiliency and gentleness. His life has taken him through a BA, three MA degrees, a PhD, a black belt in a martial art, and two Fulbright professorships. He has taught in a variety of higher education settings: large state universities, small liberal arts colleges, community college, in prison, and abroad in universities in Finland and Greece. He has published five books of poetry and over 50 individual poems in journals in the USA and abroad, as well as scholarly essays. He lives near the Monongahela River, with his wife, Amy, and their Labrador Retriever named Ella Blue.